Soil of Myself

Soil of Myself

Ian Crittenden

‘

CRANKY CRAKE BOOKS

First published in 2022 by Cranky Crake Books
1284 Sandy Creek Road
Quorrobolong NSW 2325

ISBN 9780646867076

**NATIONAL
LIBRARY**
OF AUSTRALIA

A catalogue record for this work is available from the National
Library of Australia

Acknowledgements

'Red Soil Elegies' was first published in *Now You Shall Know:
Newcastle Poetry Prize Anthology 2013*. 'Facing the Obelisk / Locals/
Twelve Bars Blue / Chin-Chin /Drinks' and 'Colasion' were first
published in *Measures of Truth: Newcastle Poetry Prize Anthology
2020*.

CONTENTS

Envoi   9

Poor Warfarin stranger   10

Glad as death   11

Facing the Obelisk / Locals / Twelve Bars Blue /

    Chin-Chin / Drinks   12

If I had a gun   20

Industrial Deafness   21

'Why is it that all of my fans are tone deaf...'   22

from Meology   23

from Meology   24

from Meology   25

Hart Crane and the Vacuum Cleaner   26

Jekyll and Hyde Park   27

Boundary dispute   28

Colasion   29

There's a bad moon on the rise   32

Plodder Effect   34

The Abstention from Sleep   35

'Would the world be better off without me?'   36

Stargazing   37

'Because I don't write ego-poetry'   38

NPW   39

Our Greatest Poet   40

Australian poetry is   41

Wine #1   42

Central Coast haiku   43

Urbane eggnog   44

The Red Soil Elegies   45

Autoplay   53

True grit   54

Some Marks for John Kinsella   55

Tinea   56

Dumbstruck   57

Why are we   58

When you leave   59

Idioms   60

This is that guy   61

Few suffice   62

Diet   63

Treasonable Doubt   64

Hobby   65

The Well   66

Seance   67

Crossing the Williams at Paterson   68

Tease of a Clown   69

Things I Hear   70

The day before the conference   71

Islington Pastoral   72

The geology underlying   73

The houso of fame   74

Mister Ethics   75

Why John Kinsella is   76

Leaves of Arse   77

Harold Bloom on a Stick   78

Envoi

Go little book, musings of a wastrel,
may you lodge up some poet's nostril.

POOR WARFARIN STRANGER

Oh, where to start, where to finish.
Everything's broken, gone bung
and wrong. The sky falls down among
the trees at the back. You go away
for years and make it big (ha ha: fat,
more like), come back and act
authentic and think you've turned class
on its arse, which you have, but not
in the way you thought and you have to verify
your ID at the embarrassy. But that kind
of talk makes me nervous. Let me share
my earthy and uncomplimentary opinions
with the Doctors of Velocity, over drinks
with that delinquent from down near
Deniliquin. He tells me, without saying
as much, that I'm just another wavering
wayfarer running low on warfarin
because of all the clots.

GLAD AS DEATH

Death is horrible but at least it isn't mine, she thought-guffawed.
Death is horrible, but freedom.
I will tell you death is horrible when I think you need to know.
Death is horrible but you can now attend a funeral.
Dancing is permitted now at weddings, no dancing at funerals.
Death is horrible but construction needs clarity.
Death is horrible because all those ghastly elegies, they amateurise grief.
Death. Death is horrible. Death is.
Death, dull-toned, unchimely toll.
Death is horrible, the photo-op trolls. Just look at it.
Horrible death is going nowhere until there is no breath.
Death, Death, Death, that horrible cardigan in the courtyard, Death,
you slow-mo bugger, you life-fugger, rolling out on the red carpet.
Death, you're horrible but take them, not me.
Death, you're horribel, but picnics, they are so lovely. Behold the river-
side willows.

FACING THE OBELISK / LOCALS / TWELVE BARS BLUE / CHIN-CHIN / DRINKS

The Oriental, The Cricketer's Arms, Cooks Hill

I sober up from drinking in the Oriental and get drunk again
in the Cricketers Arms, arriving home sometime after midnight.
I've lost my keys, I knock and there's no answer.
Spook's nose is already thundering.
I wander up the hill, and deflect the surf's applause.
For a long time I've hated this body. It's not my own,
it runs around as if it had no final destination.
Late at night the breeze is still, the ocean a phosphorescent weave.
From this time on I'd like to be a small dinghy
floating off the continental shelf, reading the currents.

Basement on Market Street, Newcastle

Bad wine, bad men. You can't get away
quick enough. Both bring me to my knees
with their promise of pleasure ruined
by stinking compromise. The moon is in pieces
on the gauzy river. The pubs are empty,
intensive care is full. I water the bed of vegetables
with my reeking piss. Spook snuffles
among the dandelions and chilli.
Such abundance, but nothing I can eat.

The Wicko, Wickham

Bad poets are like bad wine. They stick
in your craw, a fishbone swallowed backwards.
I can't not go through with it,
I just have to go on gagging.
If you see me drunk at the poets' pub,
don't slap me on the back.
Just let me pass out, then wake up
sober as the cleaners go through the place.

Sunnyside Tavern, Broadmeadow

It's Grand Final eve and I have no family near,
but I have tears like Gary Martine's sweat.
Since there is someone who burns up the street,
I can only presume that life goes on.
I imagine the two teams toss
and turn in their anticipatory dreams.
Tomorrow, the shield will be lifted,
the battered champions and their drunk fans
toasting the dwindling moon, the dying stars.

The Empire, West Newcastle

I never could keep my big trap shut, bragging
over a schooner in the Empire. Smokes
and tats could never get enough of that flatulence.
Now I've really got something to trumpet:
the critics all think I'm a dickhead! Well,
that's the turd calling the cowpat dirty. Bring it!
I've only got this glass of wine, now,
hedged between me and eternity.

Horseshoe Beach, Newcastle East

A six-pack and baited rod on Horseshoe Beach:
I'm blind again from our river's shimmer,
the ochre sunlight athwart the silos.
The tide runs in, my hooked prawn drifts,
the talk is of the filling morgues. There's another
six-pack in the esky, we're not leaving
until it's gone. The ferry shuffles to Stockton
then back across the abject harbour.
Even through my regret, studying the Way so late,
I'm just as good at composing poems as them.

Home. Islington

The ambitious canary wants to suck seed,
I just want to suck piss and toast the tree frogs
in my back yard. They're kicking up a fuss
again, with a call like a brush tail possum.
The full moon carves out my shadow
which wobbles against the wall. It toasts
me. The moon? A passing cloud dissolves it.

Foghorn Brewhouse, Newcastle

What is the use of so many nearly identical beers?
What is the true minutiae of difference?
In the great transformation, a virus becomes almost human,
one beer becomes a conversation, another turns into
the fish escorting an orphaned supertanker home,
the coal in the supertanker ends up back in a leaf
in a dying forest. Drink up, there's work to do!

Town Hall, Waratah

Three mobility scooters confer on the path
outside the Town Hall. Inside, Waratah's rising aldermen
debate the day's urgent questions.
Who is to say they haven't found the Way?

Lass O'Gowrie, Wickham

Washing my son's hair
in the tapwater at the back of the Lass
I hope that he grows up a talentless drunk,
unlike me, whose little shard of talent
has just made me miserable.
I read their poetry but can't understand a word.
I want my son to be stupid, so he can be raised up, too,
high on the vertical banners of praise!

Hunter Valley Wine Tasting, Lovedale

What are the clouds doing behind the screen
of mountains? Is it smoke piled into burning cumulus,
falling on the plain as ash, as black leaves?
The sun, also, has dropped there,
Light from some headlamps needles down,
suggesting a way out through the hairpins.

Cellar Door 1, Pokolbin

In the witching hour, when I climb inside
the third bottle, I think of that lickspittle
megalomaniac who places his head in the laps

of the powerful, then flaunts their praise
as he climbs ever higher, showing his naked arse.
Keep climbing, ant! May your ambition give you
comfort, even as it suffocates the rest of us:
I read your poetry, dull dishwater,
so cold even the suds have fled. The jonquils
at the cellar door keep blooming.

Kooragang Island

'All the cunts are at the festival
listening to the other cunts read. Poor me,
oh watch me wringing my hands, oh watch my cock
expand as I recite myself. I'm seeing them off
from Kooragang, watching the white egrets
hatch. No regrets here, just the heartbeat
of crickets, the exhaling cloud of gnats,
the mozzies as annoying as those poets',
is what he was reported as saying,
ripping another can of bespoke beer open.

Hexham Bowling Club, Hexham

Birds strung out along the fence
pass for heads on pikes at the edge of town.
The creeks, the rivers, are broken.
Wire between the poles, the palings, twangs.
Choreopsis mocks the freeway with its laughter.
I drive through it, drunk again and surly.
I've ditched my gods for the book of shadows,
and if the index is anything to go by
I'll soon be arriving in hell.

Hunter on Hunter, Newcastle

At Hunter on Hunter midnight's acoustic
duo pretend to take requests and each
sip from a middy of wine: him white, her sparkling red.
A short, angry emperor bustles out on his phone,
dark tarmac hissing with Marly wheeze and soothed
with slow blinkers, arcs from his red-boxed milds.
Ancient tunes trickle onto the street, wind kicks
around a juice box. Will I ever get to see your face again?

Belmont 16 Foot Sailing Club. Belmont

Past the Sixteen Footers, small boats,
skip under the Watagans' long shade,
a hundred, it looks like – my mounting
drunkenness, my balance all shimmy.
The handrail glints, still, and the distant
carpark's disdain manifests as rain.
Back inside, then, leave the forecourt.
Mind sails south a moment, past Swansea.

The Windsor Castle. East Maitland

They always say they want the best
for the kids, and fret over measures
of intelligence. My brain and its, um,
'chemistry', have screwed my life up.
Look instead at the sudden mill of cash
at the Bradford, the Windsor Castle –
these snotty cherubs, will they inherit dot coms, soft
drink domains, run for a seat on the Council?
You know they will, so why bother asking.

The Premier Hotel, Broadmeadow

Each bar performs my sadness. It crescendos
by design. I philandered widely, a lover in every port.
'I'm only attracted to strong women. But then I get scared
and run away.' I cracked open families
to egg myself on. Now I'm exiled from this town
by my tastes. On the way out, there's The Premier,
that pub at the sharp end of the Nine Ways:
the first stop always ends up the last.

Cellar Door 2. Pokolbin

This morning's glary frost on the couchgrass,
the bare queue of Pokolbin's poplars.
Stay inside, unless: we're all hermits now.
Who do I talk to? Is messenger even secure?
These books of his – are they saying what they seem
to say? I'd drift deliberately west, but how, and how
would I know what was waiting there? The hungry wastes.
What use are peers, friends, family, so far apart?
A thousand years of quarantine, thirty of drunken exile.
Wipe down the glass, look through the window.
I started out late, a little unadvantaged. So?

The Delaney, Cooks Hill

What the world has taken away from me
has been given back to others. Just accept it,
it's easier that way, I don't want to work
I just want to drink, plunder a book in the midsummer shade
of a lazy park or garden. Eventually, those words
will drift off into cirrus, stratus, cumulonimbus

freighting themselves inland. For now, though, the drought
continues, cremating the continent, doubting species
into extinction. How I wish I could gently stab
the faces of all the climate change deniers –
not that it would make much difference. It's a party-
political knife-fight: instinct, gut. I'll stay the course, implacable.

General Roberts Hotel, New Lambton

Wine in the sunshine, flicking between sutras
and *The Best Australian Poetry 2011*.
I walk down to the gully, watch the light
drift past the flash of wild orchids. How little
ambition I have, how fun it is having it, and how
awkward it sometimes is, not explaining it well.
People rate Lambton Heights, the view,
but I'll sit here in the front bar window.

The Albion Hotel, Singleton

I don't mean to, but I claim the bottlo's
back alley with this stinking piss. Steam rises into
that winking slot of neon and mist drops
up into first light, dawn's river's swash.
How many times have I come this way
against the afternoon's streaming sun, slinking
down lanes, avoiding those chattering neighbours.
Am I so settled in my ways? I've wet my feet.

IF I HAD A GUN

I'd shoot the poet who asks 'one more?' then reads another ten
I'd shoot the poet who puts his head in my lap and says that he adores me
I'd shoot the poet who writes the blurb for the other poet
     who gives him fifty pages in the journal that poet edits
I'd shoot that poet too
I'd shoot the poet who brings out their selected poems selected from just
     two books
I'd shoot the poet who calls themself a leading Australian poet and flies to
     the USA to talk about their poetry but hasn't published a book in
     fourteen years
I'd shoot the poet who calls the bomb squad when they receive a 'suspicious
     package' in the mail which turns out to be the ashes of their latest
     book, burned by their enemy
I'd shoot the poet who takes the piss out of any poet except me
I'd shoot the poet who carries around a word like a trophy they won in a game
     of 'who's got the biggest dick?'
I'd shoot the poet who says, 'but you can't break up with me, I'm a poet!'
     then writes about their last dud fuck
I'd shoot the poet who writes beautifully about beautiful things
I'd shoot those beautiful things too while I'm at it
I'd shoot the poet who bleats about the other poet who wins all the prizes
I'd shoot the poet who wins all the prizes too
I'd shoot the poet who doesn't know how to scan a line
wait, that'd be just about all of them
well so be it, let's shoot them all
they're just a bunch of poncy hairdressers anyway.

INDUSTRIAL DEAFNESS

I'm sick of the industrially deaf
I talk to in my local. 'What's an ego-system?'
they ask, eyeing me like the wanker
they'd like to pulp. Lately I've taken
to carrying a pen and writing down
'sandy loam' and 'overlaying yellow clay'
and the big one, 'reclamation'. Even
here I am that lone voice in the desert
of this pub crying out, a heartbeat
away from collapse, parole, dissection.

In reality, I know nothing,
just forms and how to write
a email that doesn't say
'I've got a case of the heebie-
jeebies' or 'go take a flying fuck
at yourself, denatured dipstick.'
I don't know how I keep down
a job, food, my raging hard.

They ask me about my ego-poetics
but when I talk about rehabilitation
they say, 'what? you don't look like
the ice type, you still got yer teeth.'

'WHY IS IT THAT ALL MY FANS ARE TONE DEAF...'

Why is it that all my fans are tone deaf,
charlatans, or puritans? Is it me? No.
All those poets of wit and affect,
wearing their hearts on their sleeves
drive me into a paratactic fury.
Don't they know that I am the future,
suturing their fontanelles to their parietal
lobes? My meological Parnassus
will surmount their puny achievements
like Victor Mature standing on top of
a pyramid in that movie I saw once.

FROM MEOLOGY

no.1043

Atavistic bazookaform multifoliate
espresso conforms to my immediate
Neapolitan edginess hypervivid sausage
(vegan) the indeterminacy of leaves
me up cthulhucene wilderness altars
the landscape of loaves, sourdough,
inured in the ullage of sunlight
silos silos silos and silage ant-
I pasture antipasto nuns
coruscate on a step-ladder
misophonic stepson banish
my ten-thousandth poem revealed
itself just now even my shadow
is great the shadow poems the ones
I have not yet written all bear my
watermark treadstone omniscient
haruspication solidified paratactic
obstruction where is that prune juice
lines of capital quasi-queasiness
conglomerate astrophil and stellar
networks scintillate in obsidian
ignorance the world must bow down
to me poematic pneuma of the forty
third solenoid in my breadbasket

FROM MEOLOGY

no. 512

arachnoid coruscations behind my eyelids
are a public health policy treehouse
I calculate the curvature of the earth
in my underpants $E=mc^2$ that's too easy
Mick Jones disagrees by degrees
orgones irradiate my little ethical Helmut
Ernst radishes in my Hügelkultur garden
protactinium hydrate dopplering
the purple shadows groining my gums
devolve into crows that's too easy too
little eagles are beyond moral and legal
the soil is unethical, colludes with the aliens
my middle name is Mulder and I'm older
than yesterday's men my son tells me
long distance despite the lawyers' advice
'Woolly woolly' is French in the playground
I see red in the fiery dairy air red is fast
it fixes to objects dogs don't learn object
permanence but brown is faster watch out
here it comes

FROM MEOLOGY

no.8564

Gibbet speggle acrostic
jabberwocky my new New
Testament hybrid epic is
disobedient, linguistically
speaking of which I think
of in what my greatness
consists is $P(k) = Z(k)^{-\lambda}$
or maybe it's my negentropic
glitter even Rigel or
Betelgeuse will bow down
to my brilliance, bad luck
if you think it's not for you,
it's for you, with a mesostic
blazon personally tailored
just for you with a debt
garnisheeing plan in units
of admiration called poemes
when I was born I had
constellations of poemes
swarming through my system
the doctors had never seen
anything like it I composed
my first work at one day old

HART CRANE AND THE VACUUM CLEANER

How easy we have it today. We scan for ourselves
Tingly for Him and Her and avoid altogether
the shame of being sprung buying vaso
at the corner shop by an overly-observant
school-chum. But Hart Crane... what made him
want to come in the tube of his mother
's vacuum cleaner? What model was it?
And what exactly did she say, when she found him,
dick blown by a whining electric device,
that electric screech his first, his primal muse?

JEKYLL AND HYDE PARK

A break from journeying west,
my time on the dirt magazine,
the little journal,
was unremittingly brief,
stocked with buried grief
Sydney Grammar's midday stammers
over the sandstone's plagioclase glamours.
Silicate doesn't get its due
in the work it does holding the city
together through its Miocene turbidities,
the events tongued, tied science
tides itself toward. Tidy, this place isn't.
Look at those boaters. SHS, 1993,
AM expedition. Three of us got 'lost',
campt out in the ferns, fernicating
ourselves to sleep. That one was hard
to explain.

BOUNDARY DISPUTE

We took the lillipilli down and the silver wattle too
because the neighbours worried over fire,
and pollen on the laundry,
and insisted we go halves.
So I paint the trees we lost in outline
on the blue colorbond fence and hand them
the Bunnings receipt.

COLASION

There's fuckery afoot. The street I want to turn into
is blocked off by a police car, bi-flashing-polar.
An Imperial Stormtrooper helmet, a Corolla
hatchback hurries past the boarded-up Town Hall,
away towards the stunted pines lining the oval, receding
then disappearing into dusk. Leaflets blow in a data-storm
and the last fingers of sunlight strum
the trees, the fences, in air as moist as a sea.

Black clouds, spilt toner.
Rain gauzes the next suburb.
It's nearing the middle of winter:
pigeon-hued clouds border Rorschachs
of depressive cumuli, squat on the tree-lined horizon.
It's a patchwork of cold inertia, of darkening
and damp fustiness: my mind
is the business blowing through it,
the apophenic shapes, fragmented puddles.

Apophenic shapes in a hoarsening shit storm
appear in the headlit haloes of trees. The view
from forty thousand feet is a kind of corporate catascopia:
those shining crowns, the rising steam,
the ant-work of traffic and cold cubes of tofu
and at the edges, on the post-industrial fringe,
waves release a thistling spray above
the redacted shapes of silvery shadows.
And, to the west, the crimson rim of the dying world
where corporations end, and grow back, up, and out.

Endlessly, the corporations lattice the city
to which I return like a dog to its vomit.
There's rain thick as shredded documents

shaken from windows, filling the street,
and the faint stink of entitlement thwarted
as businesses collapse like The Compaq Stadium.
Snails riddle hydrangea leaves, making green colanders.
Stars seed the night with their ancient capital.

Ancient capitals lit with neon, smoke and bandwidth.
Should we dismantle poetry now, and will it be replaced
with something better? How do we put it back together?
Fucking in the afternoon, drinking margaritas,
and eating margheritas, and reading The Master
and Margarita and licking the jade tableware?
The aim is to go nowhere, while going everywhere.
Spring is pilling Laman Street's empty trees
which nod in disagreement with the wind.

Nodding disagreement, the small child glowers,
a malevolent robot chomping empty air.
A fake American accent is quite common
among children, anal is preferred by adolescent boys,
giving mainly, but receiving also,
and then there is the Beresfield Bow-tie
and the sexual possibilities of they-on-they.
Legs spread, hands on the roofs of their SUVs,
the callow knowingness of hoodied housos, searched.

Out of the houso place, hauling the filing cabinets whole,
holding their heavy lives, the officers look just stoked.
Unshredded lives are shredded, a fist to the solar plexus,
suspect foliage drenched in the flexing rain.
There are older fragmentations not to do with age
but fortitude, the self that does not heal
but calves in the sun like a glacier
sun-pricked and collapsing into the sea.

The sea collapses against the sea wall and again
inside itself like a party or a calendar
from a cooler year, rotting out in the shed.
Mushrooms burgeon on the lawn, the pine bark
molders and the soldier ants flense a desiccated skink
so that all that's left is tinnitus and air.

Tinnitus and rain: wet sirens
blocking the street at each end. Laundered
leaves flash blue and red in the darkness.
The sky's tattooed with scattered clouds
empurpled by the city's glow, plump with rain.
Each square of the footpath is promising as an empty cell
in a spreadsheet. A Rum Corps meditation.

A quick bundy and coke as the tattooist skitters
her art across their skin: a verse from the Koran
or a headline from *El Telegraph*?; it's possible
those characters spelling bàndītóu
could mean 'lower your head in manure';
the purple blush on plumpish thighs
is just for you. My only tats:
on the backs of my eyes, the profit
and loss, the liability, limited, of Colasion.

Strelitzias and chaos: rising inequality
in these planters filled with weeds. Artless
frontages promise no more
than a co-star spot in the magnitude of space
with a cheesy credit, a string of nothingness.
Rain beads on the tricolor paddywagons.
I suppose I'll come back later, take a long ride
on my murdercycle. I might reconsider my position
on brand awareness, risk aversion,
their artful collusions, evasions.

THERE'S A BAD MOON ON THE RISE

1

I measure eternity on my own terms, thanks – my tumescent temerity
inches into each lover's lie, but shrinks when it swims.
I wanted to write this in couplets, but I went on and on far too long,
stroking time's wildness, taming her to the end. My end.
Everyone's a wanker, under the sun. I'm habitual, it's in my temper.

2

The jig's up. It was long ago.
I called bullshit on the naturalistic images
of the moon casting horse shadow,
that blood-red stallion satellite
bending the tides and us. I'm pure satyr.
I try to bed the apocalypse's horsemen – meow.

3

My cerulean mood, my pacifist children are palimpsests
for my diction's blown cogito. We move our dining plates tectonically,
but that came to an ultimate closure as I taught every -ology
even as the sun blasted open after two more billion years
of my write-wrighting wombat rites: who do I want to strangle?

4

At last! I'm here, my love. I am where I was, death lurking
less than ecstatically in judgement of the blissfully blind believers, the living on
Fools, who woke me? Fred Flintstone had cast off his toga, and Wilma's.
I fled – I'm no paleolithophile. I'm always running off.
Children weep to hear me recite. What I tell them, they can never know.

5

I've been sprung now, spring and all skulking away past the oxbow,
more fark than lark. An immiscible variety of waterbirds mingle physically.

The one more thing budded into the dampening ring of disclosure's
clenched bark and bolt. My silver streaks are quite popular
but not contrived. The poets know I say things twice
for what I think's effect. The poets know it.

6
I lived my life in a pair of Docs, thinking of pussy as fucks swing by
as if I were not quite a god, as if I were not in actual control. My life is
cosmetic, my oeuvre pancaked on thick, stucco on the walls of my cosmos.
You do what you do, don't you? Did Rod McKuen say that? I don't mind him.
What fakery pays for the house, the cars, the chipped gravel
in the long bright circular drivel? Don't think I don't practise with mirrors.

7
He would've had an entire retinue to see
to his yard, even if thanks never reached them.
O, someone to do the lawns, lop the avenues of eucalypts
wicking to the homestead, another to turn through
the endless DAs, get across local government's rituals. Me,
I'm always cutting somebody's grass – I hope I don't smell
too bad. O, rubbled cairn of marriage, time burbles onto whatever eternity is.

8
It's afternoon again, curtained by haze, rain.
The muted scent of Cannabis sativa rolls across the hills of my desire
as the colour my ancestors' farming skills stripped away
returns to country. Water again in that billabong
covers the bleached white wedged between rocks.
What hasn't become excess? Why would anyone try
to make more of this than it is? Oh, blue wren, little
bird, when will you love yourself as much as I do?

PLODDER EFFECT

Funny how the shit coming towards you seems more shrill
then the shit you leave behind in your wake. What have I done?
When I published my fiftieth book I felt the chill breath
of mediocrity blowing up my trouser-leg: 'Look on your latest work
and despair,' it seemed to say, 'you can't go back
and make it good, it'll just go plodding on.
And on. And on. Generations have plod. And plod.
Get used to it, it's like you've joined a sect.
They've got a name for it: the Plodder Effect.'

THE ABSTENTION FROM SLEEP

I know a poet who has an opposable toe.
When his hand gets tired from writing he knows where to go.

Apparently he also has a detachable head.
He leaves it dictating poems and goes to bed

but I also happen to know that he never sleeps.
The poems he writes awake will make you weep

with laughter. Or hang yourself from the rafters.

'WOULD THE WORLD BE BETTER OFF WITHOUT ME?'

Would the world be better off without me?
I guess I'd leave your garden hose alone:
these days ceramic bongs rule. I'd also leave
your idiot cultural icons alone: Nick Cave,
that dick on a pseudo-Catholic stick,
Tim Winton, Australia's leading YA novelist,
need I go on? I could bury my head
in a bucket of goon, and only Spook would miss me,
or drive into that Duckenfield tree where the road
bends but I might not. String me up
by my convictions and I will be remembered:
the fool who got it right, or the wise failure?

STARGAZING

The milky way at night:
luminol on her face.

Ace!

'BECAUSE I DON'T WRITE EGO-POETRY'

Because I don't write ego-poetry
or nourish the spirits of middle-aged pussy
with deathless spurts of Parnassian jism;
and since I still possess a dick
and stopped wearing dresses years ago
and I don't stuff my lines with mellifluous
merkins, or Bel Canto birds
painted on Persian miniatures;
and since I don't know the language
of oysters, can only speak of their grit,
nor wobble in my solitude, and even though
I've not heard of the Peruvian hyperrealists
nor translate bouffant hairdo as boofhead
weirdo; despite all this, I still dare
to call myself a poet, albeit without readers.
What's new? I get pleasure by calling it
as it is. If you happen to overhear me
pleasuring myself thus, don't call the police
but listen.

NPW

My net personal worth is less than the price of a house
in Rooty Hill. That makes me a poet. And it makes me ill.

Our Greatest Poet

That dickhead thinks our greatest poet is him:
posting facebook pec pics in the gym.

Here's some tips to help him with this aim:
don't write poems like this that scorn and maim;

write drivel by the latrine-load, then make deals
to publish them before the shit congeals.

Don't write anything good, it takes too long;
besides, some jealous hack will say you're wrong.

AUSTRALIAN POETRY IS

Australian Poetry is state politics
without an ICAC. Think of fisting millions
into dazzling Dazza's change pocket, or he
who must be Obeyed hanging on to his 30 mil.
Who would resign tomorrow on principle?
Over a TV, a bear or a goonful of Grange?
It's a little like clapped-out, put-out
never-has-beens hanging on
to that annual anthology appearance
in *Australian Poetry's Got Talent*
hosted by Rod McKuen's latest
incarnation, a dickhead with a predilection
for posing nude with cellos. I digress.
I mean, whatever happened to elan,
Frank O'Hara? We've had charisma
bypasses all along the land.
The kid who makes the biggest mess
gets the most attention. Noice.
But let's make that fucker clean it up.

WINE #1

Drink – does inhalation count? I mean by that
a bottle that disappears inside an episode
of *Game of Thrones*, or *Ru Paul's Drag Race*.
I often wonder what it's like to have a dick
when you're presenting otherwise. Is that like
Nick Cave or Paul Kelly as a poet,
or am I being mean? Of course I have a dick,
it's what makes me what I am. Like my poems,
doesn't it?

CENTRAL COAST HAIKU

Julie's bongwater
has leaked onto the pile
of poetry books

URBANE EGGNOG

Dissent in the corner at the reading because I bone on far too long,
in particular about my mediaeval AF ideas of romance –
the poets sip their surly drinks, giving me the side-eye,
a swamp rat Darth Vader.
                         I'm honest, at least,
wisecracked about breaking etiquette in their stolen time.

2
Shitness. I'm being watched – I suspect I might not
be big game. My fake dharma, saying there's nothing to say –
as if, man. My phone tolls out on incoming prank calls
I don't know how to stop. My floopy hair, my enumerated
lists of cosmic minutiae, serious trivia.
The moon irrupts from the silver-wet meaningful gutter.

3
There's no aphrodisiac like Louise's petit bourgeois oysters.
I shucked her one, in a park by the winking, nudging harbour.
Clowns in power dispense prizes of petering renown
as I pick fights. The world is the world. Word. You'll keep,
in the manner of prawns' heads in the long bin of summer.

THE RED SOIL ELEGIES

1
Again there was no winter, and summer was a similar story,
        a wet dryness, a moist drought.
                Like tiny grenades of colour the parrots explode

in trees, gleaning through sparse harvests.
        I saw two bluewrens, the male
                like Holbein's wasp-waisted Death, dancing

as the female watched, beguiled. We're like that
        with the climate, but what we get is weather.
                A wreath of red destroys the blue horizon,

I find the clean curvature agonising,
        reminding me of all that we've destroyed,
                the lean remains best left alone but still

commodified and packaged, strobed, scoped, skiied,
        and what is worse, perved on from the open air
                with signage modulating our behaviour.

2
Each wake is a hyperlink of foam or etchings
        in a cloud chamber, long wet carbon skiprints.
                I can see them all overlaying each other

like equations in a splintered light
        with no sense of how they appear and reappear,
                except as a palimpsest of indifferent destruction.

How long this wet machine will last is anyone's guess,
      but when the sun is crowning
           and the day dilates in wild blue

happiness is a normal distribution:
      aureoles of light get trapped in trees,
           the parrots rise towards, but get no further

than a wingspan of harm between the feeder and the fed,
      the hopper and the crow,
           scared by a windbreak into a black compliance

with weather. Each time I settle into contemplation
      beyond the economics of fear and isolation,
           my thoughts are fractals, stitched into order

and electrical impulse. I understand that heavy industry
      can achieve a bleak, raw beauty.
           Intervention is a two-edged word:

I have broken the code of abstinence
      yet remain in thrall to the aesthetics of the bottle,
           not its contents, over-proof

as a weeping poppy bulb harvested for the vein.
      And now, because ambition is in the blood
           I decline an invitation to be on a board

and accept another, to read - I can't help it –
      it goes to the head. Anything is better than loving words
           and not being seen or heard.

3

In the gully last summer we found toxic garbage –
    a spill of cathode ray tubes, a freezer with
        its doors blown off, the twelve-gauge

perforations gone to rust, and as though
    it had been left as a joke, like some taunt
        against the way we live, a bag of offal,

stretched to bursting point as if the plastic itself
    had been a vital organ, blown out
        of proportion by the heat.

We lined the tail-gate of the ute with a groundsheet,
    covered ourselves, and worked with pitchforks
        and by hand. Useless to try and put a name

to this wretched handiwork. Out here, our personal
    politics are public and are open game, and there
        will always be someone to load a rifle,

dump rubbish, murder animals or worse.
    Our daughter kept asking Who would do that?
    Who would come?

Sometimes you don't have answers for questions
    you know will return, fleshed
        with more detail, in the future.

4

On a morning when the soon-to-be-dead have gone
    from rehearsal to prayer, annexed
        by a kind of cynicism, I bypass the departed

and fix a loose connection between hope and despair.
    I read aloud from the *Field Guide to Loss*
        and hear weather reports in a filling

and then, out from a wetlands hide,
    my father's voice around a boxwood splinter:
        Bad season old mate – this was when time

was hand-rolled, with a feathered wedge blowing over
    gun-metal stanzas.
        When order broke there were

soft-mouthed retrievals, clearances.
    You don't have to be all things to all people,
        my father wrote, his hand coming apart.

Underwritten with belief, you can slip through,
    you can outlive the act but not the hurt.
        Too late, I followed the drop-off

into the cold upwellings of withdrawal.
    The dead, the dying were everywhere.
        Some came back after being shocked awake

CLEAR
    others scattered, and always there
        was my father, looking on through a film

of lanolin, the smoke-rings of lesions
    taking hold in the perished bellows of his lungs.
        I kept going under,

I did not know how to surface, my skin
    a winding sheet of erosion, my thoughts
        like crop-rotation in cadmium dirt.

After he died, I returned to palm ash
      into a garden iron-barked with sleepers –
         a formality he hammered home,

along with his advice on how to make love,
      go the distance with one woman:
         A pairs of shoes under the bed

cast no shadows, and all
      his other euphemisms,
         his coded preparations for dying.

5
Fissures in the winding-down of time make us sick.
      The swamp gum sweats it out,
         introductions state a case

for an aerial drop of booby-trapped bait.
      A weather report is a bone scan.
         It's ekphrastic. To formalise the death

of a local ringer, she buried his tobacco
      where he died. His marker is a drill bit,
         a fence post, a windmill blade.

He was a gifted horseman, country singer.
      A feral goat's new haircut, courtesy
         of the dogs who work the back-

paddock shift - they leave most animals alive,
      trailing entrails, to weave their wet,
         red way to death, dragging their legs.

I have been out into the carbon-black night,
        trusting my way from page
                to wire barbs. Mostly I find myself

a little afraid, enlarged upon the landscape,
        dwarfed at first light.
                I travel less and less, preferring

local roads. Imagination's international.
        A vast itinerary awaits me at the desk.
                At home, my family

are the earthwire and fire inside my words.
        When I speak of grain
                in the season's broken mouth,

or how the bullets of locals
        make a sound like a long zip being pulled
                at speed, I ask: is reclusiveness worth

the potential dangers to body and mind, the tripped
        traps of emotion, the fire-break
                breached at the height of raw weather?

Yes. Better this small, close community
        than the one we abandoned.
                The dugite's head emerging

from downed timber, wild flowers lighting
        the grass of Tallering Station - here we step
                lightly, our prints dying out on the road.

6
I'm tired of talking about the years of co-dependency –
    The tick of a cooling engine
        under the capillosa. In town we speak

to the butcher, fighting our tendency to lecture.
    A lamb watches a crow
        sharpening its knife on a bark strap.

We have so many books, the walls
    of every room are lined with spines.
        My daughter quotes a Language poet

without my intonation.
    When the fires came close, we made
        preparations, we held on.

We talked of what we'd go back for
    if we had to leave as the fire flared through.
        Once it would have been the computer,

a boxful of books. Now I'd take a spring-
    back folder full of notes, my brother's
        shearing boots and the first poem

you wrote for me.
    I'm sentimental if you know what I mean.
        I love the country but I just can't stand the scene.

7
I wake remembering the sound and vibration
    of a General Electric turbine -
        another crossing, another year

under the formal lines of an English sky,
      the free-versed horizons of America.
         My passport looks like something

unearthed from the time capsule I buried
      at the back of a towering cylinder
         filled with grain one afternoon,

depressed and coming off the back of a flagon run.
      A flashback replaces the turbine drone
         and I feel something like the un-

relenting bass-notes in the chest that was always
      part of coming down off speed.
         Being clean is still a palpable

connection to the past. The body and head
      have memory. They formalise trauma.
         It's why I don't write sonnets –

contained exuberance and enforcements of order
      have the metallic reek of dropping
         acid and listening to Radiohead.

AUTOPLAY

Lighting a candle to bring back the missing child
is ambitious and staged as a moon shot.
The dogs bark each time Sandra Oh is onscreen in *The Chair.*
How does he feel, in the same ward his mother died in?
They are the youtube autoplay of stadium rock,
sloppy overflow in the Venn diagram of taste
but I no longer give an F, or any of the other letters, either.
What was a lie in June is true in spring, so watch as the weeks
scroll down across weeks, presser on presser weighting down the ends.
The silver backing peeled away from the mirror –
a rupture in something, somewhere.
But the camp followers have something to say,
tensed up and fevered in the foul airs
on the edge of the siege, their treadmarks in the dike redundant.
The only salt on our land is in the pantry.
Waiting in the shade of the hissing pines.

TRUE GRIT

Cusson's isn't up to it. A gross box of solvol cannot remove the grit
smudged hard into these fingerprints of mine –
complicit with open cuts in the bled verdancy around Singleton.
The deep red soil surrounding the basement lab on the plotted rim of Xuanwu
is the thing I most miss, not the calibrations or boss-checked numbers
columned up like piled stanzas, pillars of salt assaulted by Saxa's demand.
The School of Infantry's interdisciplinary artillery blasts
are muffled by mine expansion.
Is there still power in the Unions, Harry Hooton?
Is there blue denim in their veins?
Who is there left to ask? Divine the answers.
Divination of light on the Muswellbrook-facing dog door
lacks the history and agency of I Ching. Which way will fortune fall?
Mine, or anyone's.
So much pent-up dirt is caught under my unscrubby nails.
Is there still timid time enough to wash my hands of this.
Is that a question. I don't know why it wouldn't be.

SOME MARKS FOR JOHN KINSELLA

A for effort,
E for affect.

TINEA

Who has the better ear:
Helen Keller
or John Kinsella?

DUMBSTRUCK

I'm dumbstruck but keep talking. The words ring around recoiling
from what I am on the make on with them,
my fluid, langourous monkeying runes,
circuitous routes language trawls,
as the river runs on past here, and runs on
and turns over its extenuating syntax
of stone, infill, tributary, its languid
landscape of words labial and liable
to mistongued moral marks in the land,
where spilt waters split and retwine, whine on
over the stoned courses sun- and times-smoothed,
more polish and bright in them than heated diaries, bleated journal-
ese-worded things.
Yes, sonless I am, but the river widdles on,
narrow and slow here, urinous tint also
on the smooth folds rising to the municipal edge.
Water's elbow nudges itself out of here.
With my white singlet on, I hum and hymn out
my single-toned songlet on slung stones.
My feet slip, I fall upon my arse, arse-first into the river.
It flies and it flows.

WHY ARE WE

The morning check-in
Why are we drinking, you ask, I mean
this time?

Is it the uncollected works
of [redacted by legal] or [it would make
life difficult]?

Why not part the curtains
with the kingfisher pattern on them and
look out across the expanse of lawn
between the front step and the four-laner
you're addressed to. It's not a question, not
really.

Splash the whisky into coffee number
one of three. The double whisky chaser,
that's the fun bit.

Why not sue, settle,
claim you've won in your Engadine panic,
and wait for the nudge nudge anonymous
tap at the door? That's rather a lot of cash.
Me, yes, I'd resign over a dodgy bear
the misso 'forgot' to claim.

That,
that's poetry. And why we're drinking
on zoom.

WHEN YOU LEAVE

When you leave these little ring-barked towns,
these one pub places with their Boundary Streets,
their curfewing guffawing Town Hall clocks,
these peeling paling Tidy Towns, these out-citadels
of councils named for the bigger, hairier towns with produce stores
and dead-end grassed-over time-wrighted railheads, yeah yeah,
you don't get to come back.
Ya can fuck off with your tidy hair and
Maitland gear, your metropolitan meth teeth,
you lose yourself. That's what really hurts.
Say hello, Sandy Hollow.
Where has my kindergarden pen-friend gone to.

IDIOMS

The river walk, Rose Point Road by the park,
mist beyond the crepuscular limits slings
itself up from the frosted-over spread of clover,
stims itself across the night-gleamt tarmac,
the roved-past river road mapped in my mind.
This landscape, so inflected with spirit –
bourbon, absinthe, mid-range rum.
There is E. coli in the language, in its
innit local idiom. There's dirt under my nails.
These clowns, research for them's baleen.
Never let it be said of Craig and Clive
that they were gutless spivs.
Who was it who was once called an arsehole?
Strap yourself in for the ride: you'd better
hope the upholstery's nice or at least a bit,
even if surprisingly, even pleasantly, ironic.

THIS IS THAT GUY

This is the guy who smarms and smirks
and wonks his sliming charm while working through
the optics of your kneecapping:
the great, generous review shows he knows nothing.

Sidle up beside him, on-screen, or off?
You get token for a ride.
Strap yourself into the background,
the flawless foreground's his, under his I.

FEW SUFFICE

I am multiple, spun off myself, so I advocate
for all my selfs – mark, too, my many words
where few suffice, when place, pace, space
splinter all into wise linguistink cracks as we teach
ourselves the souls' geographies, the loads
of country we are, the be-crowed land we lately
tactically syntacticise, raving as we go on and on in one long line, deigning
to whelm over all. I write something of this in
my overalls, and out of them, painterly and free
of the me-constraining me, encyclopaedic
as Arthur Mee's regimented red spine,
backboning all the what I have known.
All in all, is that all that there is? I am all,
I apologies, am apologies, all ipologies.

Diet

Today my cousin died at work.
Fell over twice, resuscitated once.
FairWork? Eat the rich. But first you'd have to gut
and scale them and clean out all the shit,
worse than early German models of democracy –
The Diet of Wurms. There are poets that read
your mind and write grant apps to suit –
the neo-Theosophists, post-Crowleyans,
their sympathetic maggi two-minute noodles
the closest I get to snuggles with a Blavatsky or Besant –
short of enrolling in a masterclass.
Who among you is a Master.
That's a rhetorical statement, didn't you know.
I have neither truck nor Trogg with you,
wild thing, in your sonic thongs, your faux-latex chap. Flip.
Flop. Who among you masters anything much?

TREASONABLE DOUBT

I misread his name as Olive.
He is in five digits, flogging away.
Yellow posters, yellow-bellied,
yell out seried lies and plies piles
of cash for denial of [redacted as fuck].
There is a monstrous Crag upon
this bloated mount, or is he a munt.
He is a serial textual harasser – I bet
he cannot find a route anywhere and this,
this explains his resentment, his slovenly
nature-hatred. He still lives, alive,
but those arteries must be in real trouble.
By George, he will go barnanas if he reads
he is a former poet, booted from the wanks
of the underpaid legislative arsembly.
Maybe he should attend an online
marseterclarse – the payment already
covid by the AEC. I hope he dies.

HOBBY

My new hobby is crying:
at the dog videos my sister sends me,
at ads for 4WDs set atop mountains,
ridges, world famous harbour bridges,
at rescheduled Zoom meetings discussing the paper we're 'collaborating' on,
at the results of those Zoom meetings, most particularly when asked 'chase
up those footnotes, won't you?',
when I receive mail, when I receive no mail,
when I remember water-boarding school,
at the best by date of any given ready meal and which I had been saving like a
bowl of plums,
at the state of poetry and/or soil science, neglected arts,
at the state of my status in anything.
Self-pitying autumn, wait until winter.

THE WELL

The well in wellness makes me think
of Sadako in The Ring – Ringu – emerging
bile-haired from video footage of neck-tattooed,
space earringed fade-cut sooks with genuine
concerns – Totenkopfed My body, my choice
misogynists, George-enabled tossplots, manila folders
bursting with their interpretive virility,
clenched fists pumping squirm and viral load, sucked-in
by and sucking at the sav of Q, death is a hoax,
infernal plots billionaire epidemiologists wield
against like a harsh mystic sceptre
or some such.
Like some broken-limbed creeping wet thing,
dripping foul mucus, a viscous busted Jones,
out they come, beckoning ventilation,
they can all go hark themselves.

SEANCE

Poetry.
Is it a seance?
Poetry is a seance.
Commune with the dead.
Speak with dead lines, dead lives,
deaden our vile livers, deaden, deaden,
to the tune of Theme from the Pink Panther.
Poetry, dead poets, wherefore Hart thou, though?
Your passing has a Sylvia lining, which is a total fucking gas.
The lines go on and on, a non-celebrity funeral procession,
a carnival of cardigans, last decade's slacks and dirndls. Oh, poetry:
aimless, almless, mostly harmless, mostly farmless, formless, gloriously.
G L O R I A. The airways and airwaves beckon, flotation devices for madly verbing souls.
Blavatsky, O Blavatsky, where are your Tibetan Masters' masterclasses held?
Unleash me, my liege, relieve and re-leave me and let me speak only to myself.
Hello? Are you even there?

CROSSING THE WILLIAMS AT PATERSON

This bridge. It sways like a drunk as I take the Bronco across.
The Williams is a woozy shimmer, a bright house
through a flyscreen.
The stone piles where pylons strutted the old bridge up:
what troll lurks there, tempts and waylays jerks.
Use the old names, council should pay for dual language signage.
The old Marantz system pumps out Proud Mary.
The people around here are quiet Australians,
we should pay them more credence.
Crossing another bridge, the curlicued flight of the channelled water,
the diagonal struts splash their shadows as you drive, camouflaging nothing,
inked impressions on a white car, white screen, white page.
An RBT past the bend. so I quickly slide my mull away.

TEASE OF A CLOWN

The angry broadcaster – here he is needlessly weeping
and near to catatonic – quite small, actually, in a person,
away from its habitat of echoing glitched-out fury –
sobbing now, a distressed mynah, turned down even
now in all his reach, here, in this sheltered dunny by the beach.

THINGS I HEAR

At the Historical in the park, the red and the blue steam tractors
ever since there were children to climb on them in the heat.
Tonight, these two men, bitter tongues, VB fists. One says,
'But mate, you know I love you. I didn't mean to.' The other:
'You! Your love! The worst. Your love is the worst feeling ever.'
They make a crunching sound as they down more of their piss,
ruining cans of Melbourne's least most finest. You have to,
when this happens, to put your head down and keep on
heading down Bourke Street away from the mainy, ignoring on them,
the way they ride the tractors with a sudden smooching sound now,
because you don't ever know what will happen if they know you know.
Someone yells a dopplering catcall out of a late model flat tray,
Fuck her, mate, I did. Snickers and giggles from behind me.
Around the corner it is to the Motor Inn, first time back here since.
When your step-dad dies a-sudden and the neighbours implicate you,
that's when you need to get out, to fly, but report daily to the cop shop
wherever you are. Load the car you got instead of the Customline
you set your heart's desire on, ta-ta the sandy reach under the bridge.

THE DAY BEFORE THE CONFERENCE

I was standing, then sitting,
on the back step when I read the news
about the insects, and the sky
seemed to light up, so
bright and final, like a blast,
trying the motel login,
finding a WiFi network called westeros.

ISLINGTON PASTORAL

Herbs the vivid green of home grown weed
in the grocer's fridge.
Polythene food boxes – discarded – chatter their voguish menu
against the wire high school fence.
New flats pile above the corner
in carefully selected greens and blues.
They glisten in early rain, their windows suppurating with light.
Nah, yeah, we bought it off the plan.
Blue serge pants, pressed recently,
flanellette shirt tucked neatly in.
In his 70s, a French cigarette wedged in the corner of his mouth.
Outside Islington TAB, pots lean from window flats above the tax agent:
cacti, succulents, spring sprigs of jasmine blowing in my mind.
Cat wee aroma under the door spills into the stairwell of _____ Apartments.
4 o'clock hiss of spray paint or piss on walls and in the alley
the clatter of a dropped fit.
Dawn's long shadow contracts, drags the street back toward its horizon.
West, a drought, galahs spin around a tight axis over Maitland Road.
Scaffolds and cranes frame the dawn.
Kelly Gang members disguised as baristas and artisanal brewers
hack the Facebook account of Mayf Pay It Forward.

THE GEOLOGY UNDERLYING

An Australian cannon will only damage Australian Literature,
well easy to declaimeth lamely for writers
who are faithed up in the canon
of look-at-moy over-publishing. Giddy up and gawd, will you get an editor.
Make the Brits and Bloom set think yer Straya pure as and you can say
what mad shit you feel like. The cannon I'm
in is bad, mkay, all Mr Mackey, agog at the jonquils
the aliens sell out the round window today. So.
So. Ooh la la how transgressement! How embarrow
not to be moy. I sleep three hours a night.
I bug the others. Mosquitoes coil and roil
and spoil my double-pike with canonicity.
I slurp at my soy latte looking so so past the silo.
I won't allow just anyone to breakfast with me,
Stravinsky's lunch, what? Modest, I domestos poets' pests off.
Begone, O Canon, o rant I verily will of cantos and can-do promo.
Poetry's king seller: always in hock to his betters.
Canon, I erase your printer, I combust
like drought-dried wheat in your beauteous barrel
if only for a while you'll let me rest
and take a turn at pushing my barrow.
Give us a break, will ya. Strewth.

THE HOUSO OF FAME

Poetry is in public housing, all its prefab rows of low rents,
where tone's everything, where lorries trundle past David Street,
Herbert Street, all those others.
Down the street you go, the flashed colonial frontages in your peripherals,
life's a facade, a fackade I heard it sayed in the top pub, like go easy on Goethe,
after all he wasn't strained, not much, like fun he wasn't.
Pull the threads together, man, my pop said before I swung and missed,
a mere oxbow in the river of pugilism, I swung
and he smacked me hard in the kisser that had never,
not yet kissed, late bloomer, early bruiser,
but down, I digress, to the river, all young Springsteen,
and hardly poled-in before the current tore ahead and left me banked
and shanked, unthanked, unwanked, ashore but not assured. O.
Rise, crane your neck to the understructure of the bridge, the aqueous bright
flinckering, playing in the eaves.
Hitch past Vacy, river crossing after river crossing,
the earth is an aqueduct conveying cars to bridges.
I speak for neither bridge nor earth.
O song, though, of Dermosol comes to me, the dark and loamy hummed tune
Smell that fresh dirty underness. Sponge on its clean deep flood tides
compressed down past where time went.
Keep going.
Look down from the heights cramming up tectonics
above the Upper Allyn, check the salty schematics
of the farms below pinched Mt George.
Try to learn. Try to keep up, to not keep doing what we keep on doing.
Assess the form of the land, the scooped frame the river drips through.
Just do that. I bet you can't. It's all about you.

MISTER ETHICS

Mister Ethics used up all the oxygen
in the room, telling us how good
he was. But we didn't go to waste:
our skins, vellum for his books, our shit
and guts, fertilizer for his perma-
culture farm, our bones, used tirelessly
to beat the little tom-toms of his fame.

WHY JOHN KINSELLA IS

John Kinsella is everywhere.
Today I opened my packet of Sultana Flakes
and a little plastic John Kinsella tumbled out.
It was yellow.
My seven year-old daughter returned from school with a book,
What Every Child Needs to Know about John Kinsella;
a friend of mine at the University now has to teach
John Kinsella 101, John Kinsella 201 and John Kinsella 301.
Cars I see with WA number plates now say
'Western Australia: the John Kinsella State'.
Today, after lockdown ended
I was able to buy toilet paper again
and there was Join Kinsella's face
printed on each square.

LEAVES OF ARSE

There's a black hole at the heart of the Poetiverse
where a poet's sense of modesty used to be:
but 'there's more enterprise in walking naked'
said Yeats, having a tug on the Isle of Innisfree.

Our lately crowned new emperor has no shame, it seems
and dreams of a realm in which his poetry machine
keeps on and on, like one of those crude oil pumps
in Philly, spewing out that mental Vaseline

which he calls art, but merely lubricates
the interlocking grid of lackeys he calls
'critics'. But the black hole slows down time,
flattens self, empties out the hall

of self-inducted fame. O pity the naked
arse-licker who worships his own dull flame.

HAROLD BLOOM ON A STICK

When your limbs are weary, and life is dreary
and the whole world makes you sick
there's only one thing to do, face it
with Harold Bloom on a stick!

When the critics hound, like you're Ezra Pound
and they say that your work isn't schmick
there's only one thing to do, face them
with Harold Bloom on a stick!

If your name they besmirch, you can try Ed Hirsch
but there's nothing that quite does the trick
than staring them down with a baleful frown,
with Harold Bloom on a stick!

When you're down at the shops buying vegan chops
and your wallet is back in the sticks
there's only one thing to do: pay them
with Harold Bloom on a stick!

www.ingramcontent.com/pod-product-compliance
Lightning Source LLC
Chambersburg PA
CBHW031005090426
42737CB00008B/688